S0-BBD-424

THREE MONOLOGUES

CHICAGO PUBLIC LIBRARY
BEVERLY BRANCH
1962 W. 95th STREET
CHICAGO, IL   60643

THREE MONOLOGUES

Twinkletoes • Mustn't Forget High Noon • Christine

JENNIFER JOHNSTON

LAGAN PRESS
BELFAST
1995

Published by
Lagan Press
PO Box 110, BT12 4AB, Belfast

The publishers wish to acknowledge the financial assistance
of the Arts Council of Northern Ireland

© Jennifer Johnston, 1995

The moral right of the author has been asserted.

A catalogue record of this book is available from the British Library.

ISBN: 1 873687 70 2
Author: Johnston, Jennifer
Title: Three Monologues
Format: Paperback
1995

Cover: *Portrait of Jennifer Johnston* by Basil Blackshaw
Cover Design by December Publications
Set in New Baskerville
Printed by Noel Murphy Printing, Belfast

BEV

R07122 99434

For all the men, women and children who have been victims
of violence and intolerance, for so long, in this country, Ireland.

CHICAGO PUBLIC LIBRARY
BEVERLY BRANCH
1962 W. 95th STREET
CHICAGO, IL   60643

CONTENTS

Preface

People ask me, from time to time, about the process of writing. I find this difficult to explain, as it is inexplicable. I do try, though to fumble with words and to give them some sort of inadequate explanation.

I have very little difficulty, however, with these three pieces. In each case, a voice imprisoned in my head, demanded with great vigour to be let out; to be freed. I sat down at my desk and each person in turn dictated their story to me and obediently, I wrote it down.

I was reminded as I performed my task of my grandmother, a dignified, well-to-do lady, startled, I think, by the brilliance of her son, who used to sit in the drawing room of her house in Lansdowne Road, Dublin, and type as he walked up and down the room dictating to her. I may have imagined this, but I have a very vivid picture of it in my mind and I had this bizarre feeling as I write that I was my own grandmother, obeying the dictates of an unruly child.

This is, of course, daft. But then, you need to be a bit daft to be a writer.

Christine was the first of the three to impose her will on me ... and the word impose in the context of Christine is a little strong. She just manifested herself one day, across the kitchen table and spoke quietly, but with great insistence until her story was down on paper, then she went back to wherever she had come from, perhaps from some till in Marks and Spencers.

I titled her story 'O Ananais, Azarais and Miseal'. This is a title that I, personally, love, because it resonates in my head and also in my memory.

A canticle with a jolly tune and wonderful words, imploring every living thing to bless the Lord, to praise him and magnify him for ever. I was really glad to discover that Christine had the same feeling about it as I had had, all those years ago.

But the title led to problems: "Who the hell are Ananan ... whatsit and whatsit anyway?" I was asked at one stage by someone trying to struggle with such a mouthful of names.

"They were the angels who rescued Shadrach, Mishach and Abednego when King Nebuchadnezzer had thrown them into the burning fiery furnace."

"Oh ha ha."

Since then the title has slipped into becoming the pronounceable 'Christine'. I don't think it has the same ring to it at all, but she retains her integrity and that is all that matters. I wasn't at all sure what to do with Christine after she had been released on to the page.

Was this a short story?

A play?

Or what?

Perhaps just a load of meandering nonsense.

I was informed by Caroline FitzGerald that it was indeed a play and before too long it was most caringly and movingly translated on to the stage of the Peacock Theatre by Rosaleen Linehan and Caroline FitzGerald.

The BBC then showed interest, but they said they 'needed to know more' and I was in a quandary as to how to give them more without overburdening Christine with explanations, but, luckily for me, Billy sauntered into my head and both pieces were done together on the radio, most successfully.

Maybe some people will think that Billy is a little irreverent. I rather like him, however. I feel sorry for him, no one deserves to die like that, and he serves his purpose, which originally was to illuminate Christine.

Twinkletoes is the most recent of these pieces.

It was written in about a week, after I spent some time visiting the Maze prison to talk about writing to anyone who wanted to listen. I was received with such courtesy and generosity by the prisoners that I felt, after a while, I would like to write something, not about them, which would have, to my mind, been crass in the extreme, but for them. I wanted to repay in my own way these men for what they had given me during those few hours. I was thinking along those lines when Karen danced into the room and took over from me. I really hadn't much say in her creation. I merely cut out a few swear words after she had gone away and hoped she wouldn't mind.

There's not much else to say, really, except that I am glad of the opportunity for these three people to reach a wider audience than the few who go to lunchtime theatres. I believe that they will be as readable as they are watchable and I would like to think that the survivors, Christine and Karen might even get to read them too.

Jennifer Johnston
22nd January 1995

TWINKLETOES

Twinkletoes was first performed by the Project Theatre at Bewley's, Grafton Street, Dublin in 1993. The role of Karen was played by Carol Scanlan. The production was directed by Caroline FitzGerald.

It is quite late at night.
The empty living room of a small terrace house.
Light shines in from the street outside.
A car draws up, the headlights shining on the walls.
A door slams and the car drives off.
There is the fumbling of a key in the door.
The door opens and Karen comes in.
She switches on the light.
She is dressed in finery; a hat in her hand, flowers pinned to her coat, very high-heeled shoes, a shiny bag.
She is in her mid-thirties, a bit the worse for wear.
She flings her hat across the room.

KAREN
That hat cost me.
I never before bought anything that cost me like that hat.
[*She picks it up and puts it on the table. She unpins the flowers from her coat and puts them beside the hat. She giggles.*]
Tell me something, hat, I might need to wear you to the christening, so I might. On the other hand ...
[*She hokes off her shoes and sighs with relief.*]
Tell you something else for nothing, I'll not be wearing them again.
They have my feet tortured.
Our Mary always says that plastic shoes draw your feet. Well, plastic or not, my feet'll never be the same again
Nev ... er.
I'd of stayed on a bit and had a bit of crack, danced.
Yeah.
Danced.
If it hadn't been for the pain of my feet.
[*She wriggles out of her tights and throws them across the room.*]
Freedom!
[*She does a few quickstep twirls around the table.*]
I like a bit of a dance.
My daddy taught me to dance when I was wee.
Quickstep.
Foxtrot.

Tangoooo.

Twinkletoes, he used to call me.

He told me about this little kid who used to dance on the pictures.

Shirley Temple.

All curls he said and twinkletoes.

I never saw her. Only heard the name from my dad.

Some people think you're over the hill at thirty, past it. Past everything, but I have news for them.

I can rock and roll, jive, strut.

Given the chance.

A lot of other things I could do too, given the chance.

God, my head's going round and round.

Cup of tea.

I'm spinning.

Where's the kettle?

Everything's spinning.

Ya dee da da.

There it is.

God bless us.

Isn't it well tomorrow's Sunday.

Ya dee da da.

I can spend all day in bed, curtains pulled.

Tight, real tight.

Just lie there.

Let the feet recover.

Let the head stop jiving.

Cigarette. Poison.

Who the fuck cares?

A short life and a merry one.

What's merry?

I could die in my bed tonight and no one would know.

Till Thursday.

Someone would be sure to know on Thursday.

I was sure I had matches in my bag.

On Thursday, someone would wonder.

Nothing but tissues in here. A million tissues; my bloody eyes all over them.

Bin for them.

I never thought I'd cry.

Matches.

Thank you, God. At least you recognise the need for poison.

I said to our Mary this morning or yesterday or whenever it was. Why should I cry? Amn't I only too glad to be getting that problem off my back?

If I'd a had sense, I'da brought another pair of shoes with me and stayed on.

Danced.

Takes your mind off things.

Yip.

That's what I'da done.

Never had sense.

That's what my daddy always said.

He never said that about our Mary, only me.

Right enough, Danny McCartney was coming on a bit strong, but I could have handled that.

I could have ...

Just dance, I could have said and stop messing about.

I could have said that if I'd wanted to.

I called him Twinkletoes once.

One night I was out with our Mary and the girls and he asked me onto the floor.

Right enough, he was a great dancer. So I said it. I gave him that name.

There's other bits of him twinkle too.

Keep your twinkling hands off me or I'll deck you.

He laughed.

He didn't mind, not like some of the others I won't mention who won't take no for an answer.

Dirty buggers.

Only one thing on their minds.

If they had minds.

Danny's not like that.

Danny's a gentleman.

His wife's inside in the hospital.

Stuck on tablets.

Four, five years now, she's been going in and out.

Ever since her brother was shot by the army.

She just sits there, Danny says, staring at the wall.

Well, that's what he says anyway.

Lucky they've no kids.

You've no time to sit and look at the wall if you've kids.

It's her nerves is shot to hell.

She was always nervous. I remember her at school, if the teacher looked crooked at her she'd burst into tears.

We used to pull her leg.

Waterworks we called her.

I never thought I'd cry.

Tea bags.

But I did.

She looked so young.

She is so young.

And the baby showing. Maybe not to everyone, but if you knew you could see.

My daddy was affronted having to walk to the altar with her.

He said no when I asked him. Nothing on earth would make me, he said, but I said just get on and do it. Isn't she your own flesh and blood. Don't you love her no matter. I said if you don't say you'll do it, I'll have to get Declan's da down from Belfast to do it and you won't like that one little bit. That did the trick. But wild horses wouldn't drag him to the party.

He never liked Declan.

My Declan.

Not our Noreen's Declan.

He's a harmless young fella.

I thought it was an odd thing she took up with a fella of the same name.

Coincidence like.

Milk in the fridge.

Light goes on, always the light goes on. One of life's miracles.

Oh Holy God! No milk in the fridge.

Isn't that just my luck.

18

Black tea turns my stomach.

He never liked Declan from the moment he laid eyes on him.

He wouldn't open his mouth to him when he came to the house.

Eighteen years ago.

That's the waste of a tea bag anyway.

Bin.

Last week there were mice in this bin.

I got Noreen's Declan to set a trap.

Two he caught.

It's not a very nice way to kill an animal, but who wants mice in their bins.

He'd just sit there and read the paper, or a book.

Here's Declan, I'd say and he wouldn't lift his eyes from the page.

Never you mind my mammy said, he'll come round.

But he never did.

Wouldn't speak Declan's name when things got really bad.

He was in the navy during the war and he worked at the base here till the government closed it down.

You can't beat the navy, he use to say.

That's where he learnt to dance, when he was in the navy.

Joined the navy to see the world and what did I see, I saw the sea.

He'd sing that.

He doesn't sing songs any longer now.

No one to sing them to, he says now.

Who'd want to hear my songs now.

All the nice girls love a sailor. Look at your mother. She was the nicest girl of the lot. She'd go red when he said things like that.

She'd pretend to be cross, but she loved it. My Jack Tar she called him.

Do you take this man ...

That's when I cried. I couldn't help it. I knew I was ruining my eyes, but I cried and cried. Quite quietly you understand, but I used a lot of tissues.

For Declan.

I'll tell him about it on Thursday.

Not all.

I'll tell how pretty she looked and how young.

I'll tell him my daddy gave her away.
Straight and frail standing up there beside her.
Remembering. I'm sure he was remembering.
I won't tell him that I cried.
I won't tell that the baby showed.
No.
I cried for Danny McCartney too.
Though I shouldn't.
We both been alone such a long time.
What with her being in and out staring at the wall.
Not alive really.
I shouldn't think about him.
I won't mention his name to Declan.
Or anyone else.
I cried for my daddy.
He's alone too, now.
So many people alone.
I wonder if there's a drop of vodka.
Might as well be hanged for a sheep as a lamb.
He'd have come to the party if my mammy'd still been alive.
She'da made him.
You're a big baby, Sean, she'd have said.
She could have coaxed him. Wind him round her little finger.
Jack Tar.
We could have asked the band to play a slow foxtrot and he and I
could have dazzled them all. Big solo performance.
Only perhaps they wouldn't have known how to play a slow foxtrot.
What's that when it's at home? A slow fucking foxtrot.
There are pictures of him and her all round their house.
Together.
Him in his uniform.
Them being married. Very old fashioned.
Do you take this man ...
And then pictures of us all, our Mary and me.
I was the baby.
He loved me.
I was always surrounded by love.

I asked him if he'd come and live here after my mammy died.

There was just Noreen and me.

She could have slept in the room with me.

He could have been a father to her.

He said no.

He said no to our Mary too.

I want my independence, he said to her.

Your Declan's friends might shoot me, he said to me.

I didn't speak to him for six months after that.

I told Declan one Thursday.

He laughed.

Ay, he said, the old bugger, they might and all. But he didn't mean it.

He always told me not to mind the way my daddy carried on. It's just the way he is, he said.

Declan's a good man.

I sometimes wonder if he'd been here how things would have worked out.

Would Noreen have stayed at school?

I wanted her to stay at school.

Education is the only way, I said.

Way out.

My daddy said it too, and our Mary.

And her teachers.

Maybe too many people said it.

She wouldn't listen.

She wanted to live, she said. She wanted a few pounds in her pocket.

She wanted freedom.

She was growing up, she said and she wanted ...

I knew there was vodka somewhere.

A glass. Freedom.

She had her wee job in Dunnes, so what could I say to her?

Fair dos to her, she gave me a few pounds every week. Left it on the table there every Friday evening. I couldn't fault her for that.

When we were young my daddy had us in by ten o'clock.

A minute late and you were in trouble.

Maybe that's why I married Declan, so that I could stay out after ten at night.

I loved him.

Excuse me, I love him. Yes.

I think.

He's a hero.

It's hard being married to a hero.

It's a bit like being in prison too.

Don't get me wrong. I mean no harm when I say a thing like that.

Nine years he's been in there.

It was Noreen's eighth birthday when they picked him up.

At a checkpoint in Co. Tyrone.

I'd said to him that morning as he was going out, don't you be late for the wee party. It wouldn't do to disappoint the child.

Would I be late? he said, just like that, real cool. Would I be ...

We heard it on the six o'clock news. BBC.

Three men lifted.

In possession.

They showed us the car on the screen.

Jesus God, I said to our Mary, that's Paddy Breen's car.

I think they've got Declan.

Don't cross your bridges until you come to them, our Mary said.

He never turned up for the party.

I had a cake with pink icing and eight wee red candles.

What'll I say to my daddy, I said to our Mary.

Nothing, she said, keep your lip buttoned.

I knew it would happen one day.

I used to get those shaking fits.

All I could do was sit there with my hands locked between my knees and wait for the shaking to stop.

I didn't tell Declan.

I didn't want to put those sort of worries on him.

The doctor wanted to put me on tablets, but I wouldn't take them.

I'd seen what the tablets did to other women.

Like Danny McCartney's wife.

I'd rather feel.

I don't think he knew what I meant, the doctor, when I said that to him.

He just shrugged his shoulders up and down. Suit yourself he said.
I had terrible dreams when Declan was out at night. Sometimes I'd
sit up half the night just so I wouldn't have those dreams.
Our Mary said I should have taken the tablets.
She's always full of sense.
That doesn't mean she's right though.
I was too young to be a mother.
That's what I think about Noreen too.
She's too young.
What about her freedom now?
I haven't told Declan.
My Declan.
He'd be shocked, like my daddy.
Angry with me.
Why didn't you keep an eye on her?
That's what he'll say.
God knows, I tried.
He couldn't understand.
Things are so different now.
Young ones want freedom.
Nine years of changing.
He wanted freedom too.
Words are such silly things.
I'll say nothing yet awhile.
Stay mum.
I think I'll have another drop of vodka.
Someone once told me that the Russians just throw it down their
throats. Like that. Oh Jesus!
It must have been my daddy.
He was on the Russian convoys during the war.
He said it kept the cold out, drinking it down like that.
He said he couldn't describe the cold. Your breath froze, he said,
tears froze on your cheeks.
He said they used to hug you, put their arms around you and hug
you. Russian men did that. Maybe it was because of the cold.
If I'd stayed on awhile, maybe Danny McCartney would have come
home with me.

I shouldn't be thinking things like that.

God forgive me.

But I do.

Maybe he would have come home with me.

Maybe ... oh God, maybe ...

It's the drink in me talking.

No.

It's not.

I'm not a bad woman.

This house is empty now.

Full of shadows.

Noreen took all her things out of her room. Her wee bits and pieces. She left the window open and it rained and I came home and found the floor all wet and the blue rug Declan and I bought on our honeymoon in Galway. Soaking wet.

I sat on the bed and cried and she came in and put her arms around me and she cried a bit too.

We'll only be down the road, she said.

It's not that, I said. It's my blue rug.

Is that all, she said. It'll dry, she said.

So it will, I said.

It was raining the day we bought the rug and we brought it back to the caravan.

Our Mary's husband he said we could have their caravan for our honeymoon.

And it rained.

It rained like I had never seen it before.

Maybe that was just Galway.

I didn't know.

I'd never been down to Galway before.

Or since, if it comes to that.

What does it matter on your honeymoon if it rains or not was what everyone said. Nudge, nudge, wink, wink.

I'd never seen the west before.

I'd never seen the ocean.

Next town America, Declan said.

It was all white waves and seagulls.

Like kittens crying they were.

Our clothes never got dry.

Mind you the air was good. Wild air. Not like you get here.

He laid the rug down on the bed and said, ever heard of a magic carpet?

Heard of one, I said, but never come across one.

Not too many magic carpets in Derry.

Come here to me and I'll show you just how magic a carpet can be.

He was so sweet.

We didn't get to America, but we forgot about the rain for a while.

Magic carpets.

Happy ever after.

Fairy tales.

Shit, all shit.

But we tell them to our children just the same.

My daddy used to tell me about the Russian convoys and the high crashing seas and the torpedoes and the rum ration and how to drink vodka, and how the ack-ack guns sounded when the bombers came over.

He used to tell Noreen too, but she didn't want to listen.

Everything changes.

The things we want to listen to; the things we want to be.

Is she happy now with her Declan and the baby just starting to show.

She laughs. She dances.

I laugh.

I could dance.

Twinkletoes.

Do you take this woman ...

Do you take this child just starting to ...

Oh, sweet fucking shit!

I told her she had a choice, but she didn't believe me.

She didn't want me to tell her daddy.

She didn't want to tell her daddy herself one Thursday.

I hate empty bottles.

Empty.

I'd like to drown in drink.

Float away and then just slowly drown in vodka.

Russian convoys.

I had the choice.

No.

I was wild for Declan.

Even my daddy couldn't stop me loving Declan.

He's a terrorist, my daddy said.

I went out of the house and slammed the door.

The house shook.

A freedom fighter, said Declan. Tell him that. And I'm fighting for his freedom as well as my own. Tell him that.

Of course I didn't.

Tell him up the RA.

I didn't tell him that either.

I had more sense.

The people I love most all go on and on about freedom.

I don't know what it means.

I don't see it around.

Maybe you could find freedom with a magic carpet?

If you could find a magic carpet.

I made her come up with me the Thursday before last.

I'm passing no messages to your daddy, I said.

If you're getting married, you're going to tell him yourself.

You owe him that.

Since she left school, she's hardly come at all.

I can't be taking time off work to go up and see him, she said.

Excuses, excuses.

Anyway, I don't want them to know.

Anyway, I hate that bus and all those women with their plastic bags full of oranges and new jeans and the talk about our boys. And they're all so old.

And I hate the prison and the screws staring at you. And I hate ...

Don't say another word, I said.

Fuck, she said.

And don't use language like that.

You do.

I'm old, I said.

Thirty-five last May.

Coming on seventy.

Anyway the long and short of it was that I made her take the day off and she came up in the bus with me.

He was so glad to see her.

He looked great, all dressed up and his face excited with this big smile ...

I kept my fingers crossed.

He held her hand so tight, like he thought she might fly away.

You're so pretty, just like your mammy.

I sat watching them, quietly, thinking my own thoughts.

And the time flew in and she never said what she'd come to say.

So, out of my silence, I said, Haven't you something to tell your daddy?

She stopped talking and looked at the table.

She gave a little nervous clear to her throat.

I'm getting married on Saturday week.

He didn't seem to take it in.

So I repeated what she'd said.

But you're only a kid, he said.

I'm seventeen.

You're only left school. You're too young.

You and mammy were going out when she was only seventeen, she told me that.

He glared at me.

Karen ... he said.

I shook my head.

She won't listen, I said.

She'll listen to me. Won't you listen, love? You're only young. You've all your life in front of you.

I'm getting married on Saturday week no matter what you say and that's all there is to it.

She stood up, ready to go.

At least tell your daddy what his name is.

Declan. Isn't that funny. Same as you. O'Hare.

He looked like someone had hit him.

Why didn't you tell me before Karen?

I could only shake my head.

He's a nice lad, I whispered.

He looked like he'd looked in the court the day the judge had said he was going away.

I'd like to meet him, he said.

Sentences to run concurrently the judge said.

After the wedding. I'll bring him up some Thursday after the wedding.

Three life sentences to run concurrently.

If you gave a cat three life sentences, it would still have six lives left.

Or eight if they ran concurrently.

And they don't run, believe you me.

They crawl.

You might have waited till I came out, he said.

Thanks, she said. We've better things to do with our lives than wait for miracles to happen.

She turned and walked out.

She didn't kiss him or nothing.

Young people can be ... can be ...

I've done my best, I said. Honest to God, Declan ... very hard sometimes. Yes.

I know, love.

He smiled at me.

My dad's helping out with the wedding. We'll do it well. You know, the hotel, a meal, a few drinks.

Have a band, he said.

Yes.

Tell me Karen ... is she ... is she ...

No, I lied.

He believed me. I could see him believing me.

I'm quite good at lying.

Thirty-five.

I want to dance.

Jive.

Jitterbug.

Tango.

Rock.

I really want to rock.

I want to have more kids.

I want to love.

Not just on Thursdays.

Aye, Declan, I love you.

I lie well.

You've fucking well ruined my life, Declan. That's what I want to say.

And your own.

You're a hero.

Wear it well, I say.

I'm just a woman whose plastic shoes hurt.

[*She laughs suddenly.*]

I saw these shoes in a book the other day.

Pale cream coloured leather. Soft. With tiny little straps around the ankles. Not too high. Just perfect for dancing all night.

A hundred and thirty quid.

Just this little pair of soft leather shoes.

You wouldn't want to wear them in the rain.

I could do the slow foxtrot with Danny McCartney, forever.

Or someone.

He has a good job with Ulsterbus.

An office job.

Pensionable.

He's not a messer.

He doesn't look at anyone else, only me.

Twinkletoes.

I wonder if Declan knows all the things I don't tell him?

I don't want him to be upset.

I loved him.

He did what he had to do.

Even after nine years I haven't worked out what to say to him on Thursdays.

I practise going up in the bus. In my head, you know.

All the little things I'm going to say.

The jokes.

Keeping some sort of door open for him.

I often wonder if the other women are doing the same.

If Danny McCartney came over one night, would anyone tell him?
I bet they would.
Does it matter any longer?
I can't answer that question.
Not when I'm full of drink.
I don't think I could answer it when I'm stone cold sober either.
My daddy would be angry.
You've made your bed and you must lie in it, he'd say.
Perhaps we could both be a bit happy.
Laugh a bit.
Care.
Ever heard of a magic carpet, I might say to him.
I wonder what he'd say to me.
Declan sent the flowers ... and some for Noreen too. Pink roses.
Hold them over your tummy, I said, and no one will notice the way you are.
Wasn't it good of your daddy to think, I said.
She didn't answer, but she carried the roses.
Over her tummy.
She looked lovely.
My daddy thought so too.
You look lovely pet, he said and kissed her. I only hope this young lanky isn't in the same line of business as your daddy.
I could have killed him, there and then.
She just laughed.
Of course he isn't, grand-dad. Things have changed.
Amen, said my daddy.
Amen, I said, inside my head. Nothing changes and everything changes.
On Thursday I'll tell him ... everything and nothing.
I'll smile and talk about the band.
And the roses.
And the way my daddy walked up the aisle.
And about my hat and how my shoes hurt me.
Everything and nothing.

MUSTN'T FORGET *HIGH NOON*

Mustn't Forget High Noon was first broadcast by BBC Radio Ulster on 27th April, 1989. The role of Billy was played by Oliver Maguire. The broadcast was directed by Jeremy Howe.

Yes.

Yes there.

I'm just having a wee smoke.

I'm down to fifteen a day now. That's not too bad. My doctor says it's fair dos.

I used to smoke forty, but I cut it down a couple of years ago.

I used to be choked in the winter with bronchitis.

Too young to die!

I said that to the doctor.

Aye Billy, he said, *far too young.*

I just thought I'd tidy up the hedge a bit before it gets too straggly.

It's fierce growing weather.

To tell the truth, I had to get out of the house for a while and I couldn't say to her that I wanted to breathe in a bit of fresh air, so I told her I was coming down to tidy up the hedge.

You'll have the minister after you, she said, cutting the hedge on a Sunday.

She doesn't see eye to eye with our minister.

What he doesn't know won't hurt him, I said.

God will probably strike you dead, she said.

She's like that from time to time.

I went to church this morning.

I sing in the choir.

I've sung in the choir since I was a wee fellow.

My mother did before me.

It was the first church to let women sing in the choir ... that's what my mother always said.

Enlightened, she said it was.

They all do it now.

Christine couldn't come this morning, not that I think it broke her heart.

The old man can't be left alone now and we've no neighbours we can ask to keep an eye on him.

The whole house smells of sickness. It's not that she doesn't keep things clean ... not at all ... you just can't get rid of the smell. The minute you go through the porch it's there. I'd say you could even smell it off me now, if you came close.

The cigarette kills the smell.

No harm to him but it will be good to get back to normal.

It's a strain for her. You can see that. No go in her these days. No jizz.

I don't know what we'd do without the box.

She watches that a lot. She can sit there in the room and listen out for him.

There's films in the afternoon as well as the evenings and then the serials.

Takes her mind off things.

There's too much news.

That's my one complaint.

I sometimes think I'll write a letter to them about that.

Too much news.

She gets depressed after the news.

I tell her not to bother with it ... it's better to stick with the serials.

Where's the point in upsetting yourself?

I don't get upset.

I can stomach the news better than she can.

I can translate the news.

Aye.

That's what you have to do.

You have to translate everything that happens really.

Into your own language ... know what I mean?

I try to do that for her, but she doesn't always listen.

Of course it's different for me. I know my own language.

I used to go to the Field with the old man, right since the age of nothing. My mother would pack me off with him from the time I could walk. I think she thought it might put a brake on his gallop if he had to stay sober and bring me home before dawn. Maybe that's a bad thought, though.

I used to march beside him in the procession wearing a wee cocky cap over one eye with orange streamers flying down my back. He carried one of the poles of our banner.

That was a great honour. And I'd march beside him proud as a peacock. We had a great wee band here ... still do ... the

Aughnacloney Silver Band. They play all those great marching tunes.

On the green grassy slopes of the Boyne ... dedadadadadadade ...

We'd march through the village and then round and up the Back Street just the old man said to give the Taigs a tune or two ... and we'd play loud and sing loud too, so they could hear through their closed windows.

Just a bit of fun really.

I wonder does he think of those days now or what goes on in his head as he lays there?

I wonder does he see heaven as one great sunny Twelfth of July?

That man, he said to me once, pointing to King Billy on his white horse, *that man, my son brought freedom to this country and don't you ever forget it.*

His voice was filled with quivers when he said it.

I think he had a bit of drink taken.

I told Christine that one time ... oh yes, she'd made some rude joke about my bowler hat and I told her right out that she'd no call to be jeering at the Lodge. If it hadn't been for the Orange Order, we'd all be lackeys of Rome.

What's the difference, she said, *between that and being lackeys of the English?*

What's a lackey anyway, she asked then and we laughed.

One thing about her, she likes to laugh.

The old man used to take me to the pictures.

My mother had two wee girls on her hands and she was glad enough to get shut of me from time to time.

Sometimes he'd take a wee juke into the pub next door before the big film came on.

I never told her.

He knew I'd never tell her.

Men must stick together, son.

He'd come back with a bag of bulls'-eyes ... something strong like that so as she wouldn't get the smell off him when we got home.

Men must stick together, son.

I always thought I'd have a son.

It's rough to think there's no one to follow you in the world.

No one to remember you when you go.

They don't make pictures now like they used to—easy to understand.

You knew then who was good and who was bad.

It's not like that any more.

I couldn't be bothered going any more.

Destry Rides Again.

Jimmy Stewart ... a real good guy.

See what the boys in the backroom will have and tell them I'm having the same.

I remember the old man getting all worried at the beginning of the film ... shoving the sweets into his mouth ... thinking this was going to be an unsuitable one for me.

Bad women.

My mother'd be real raging if she knew he'd taken me to a picture with bad women in it.

He never said a word when we came out ... not till we got to the gate of the house and then he said *That Stewart is a great fellow. We'll tell your mother all about him. Hey?*

We'll keep our mouths buttoned about ...

Frenchy, I said, just to let him know I was clued in.

Frenchy.

We always had to tell her the story of the film when we got home, I think she'd have come with us if it hadn't been for the wee girls.

She liked to hear the stories.

We used to kind of act them out for her.

He really fancied himself as Jimmy Stewart.

He liked to think of himself as a hero.

I always had to do the bad parts. The ones who got killed. The Red Indians, the rustlers, the bad eggs.

Naw.

He let me be Chief Sitting Bull.

I won that time.

My mother never believed the Indians won the Battle of Little Big Horn.

You can't be right, she said after we'd acted it out for her.

That's history, said the old man. *That is History.*

Well, I don't think you're right, so I don't.

I don't think those savages ever won at all.

I never heard before that they won anything. It's just the pictures.

I remember sitting with him one evening watching that film ...

Custer's Last Stand and on to the screen comes this guy on his white horse and I said to him ...

Dada is that King Billy?

He took a hold of my arm like he was going to break it.

God almighty will you whisht, son. It's General Custer and don't you go making a show of me, asking stupid questions like that. Where did you get a notion like that at eleven?

I'd like to have seen King Billy on the pictures.

The battle of the Boyne would have made a great picture.

My mother always said she felt sorry for the horses.

They didn't choose, did they? To be slaughtered like that?

I don't suppose anyone chooses to be slaughtered or did they live to a ripe old age.

Or General Custer's come to that?

I bet it came to a sticky end ... out there at Little Big Horn.

Great name.

Little Big Horn.

The Battle of the Boyne.

Derry, Enniskillen and the Boyne.

The old man gave me a cowboy set for Christmas once.

A hat and a star and two holsters on a belt with shiny sliver guns in them.

I used to practice the quick two hand draw with my friend Sammy.

I wanted to wear them on the twelfth, but my mother wouldn't let me ... *where do you think you're going*, she said as I was going out the door. *The OK Corral or somewhere? You're not wearing that get up to the Field.*

Away upstairs and put your tidy trousers on ... and your nice, wee cap.

I brought the two guns with me though and she never knew Sammy and I slipped away while the speeches were on and played our own games.

Sammy was my best friend.

Right through school we were together.

He was a hard man.

Spent most of his time outside the headmasters room waiting to see him.

You could hear him in our class whistling Orange songs.

He had this real piercing whistle you could hear a mile away.

They had to take him out of Miss McMullan's class in the end, she couldn't manage him.

They put him into Mr. Barrett's class.

He managed him all right!

He was a hard man too.

I'm glad I never had to go through his hands.

Rough but.

My mother used to say ... them Barretts was always rough.

Burst two of the boys' ear drums when I was there.

Nowadays you're not allowed to lift a finger to the kids.

Mr. Barrett'd be locked up if he was around now.

Right place for him ... the Maze.

There's a lot of savages around here should be locked up.

There was no harm in Sammy. He was just wild when he was a kid ... that's all.

He settled.

Everyone settles ... given half a chance.

I stopped going to the pictures with the old man when I was about fourteen.

Went with Sammy instead.

More crack with Sammy.

We used to slick our hair back smooth and straight with water and we'd buy the odd couple of smokes and puff away.

We'd even pretend we were sixteen and pay full price.

War pictures were OK, but not as good as Westerns.

Naw.

The girls all sat together, but if you got in the row behind them you could lean forward and blow smoke down the back of their necks.

Some of them used to wear scent. Just a little behind their ears.

James Dean.

Yeah.

Good old Jimmy Dean.

The girls loved him.

I suppose we all loved him.

The old man wouldn't have liked him as much as James Stewart though.

He wasn't really a hero.

He was only pretending to be one.

You could see that in his face.

Not like King Billy Custer.

Our banner had great gold tassels along the bottom.

They would blow in the wind ... and the ropes would blow in the wind and the old man would struggle with his pole sometimes as the banner struggled to blow away. Take off.

I used to think of King Billy on his flying horse, galloping over the clouds, the gold tassels flying.

Remember, it was written in big writing.

Remember Derry, Enniskillen and the Boyne and it would fly, curling and uncurling, tassels, the flying horse, the sword bravely waving, through the clouds and the blue sky until they fluttered down to earth on top of the Vatican.

I used to have dreams like that as we walked to the Field.

Right on top of the Vatican.

St. Peter's draped with our Lodge banner ... and they'd have to find the greatest steeplejack in the world to get it down.

Custer's Last Stand.

I never said that sort of thing to anyone, just kept it to myself.

Right up to we were sixteen or even seventeen, we used to bring those guns of mine to the picture house.

We used to swagger down the road twirling them round our fingers. You know the way. That took a lot of practise.

The girls would squeal and pretend to be frightened.

God but we were very innocent then!

Do not forsake me O my darling ...

He sang that.

He had a wee brother and I gave him the guns one summer afternoon ... and the holsters. The hat was a bit worse for the

wear so I didn't bother giving it to him. I threw it in the bin.
We're big boys now, Billy, are we? said my mother when she saw it.
The lad was thrilled ... galloping off he went over the field down
to the lake.
Pkew. Pkew. Pkew. Firing to left and right.
Don't ever point them at anyone I shouted after him or I'll take
them back.
You have to tell the kids that sort of thing. The old man said that
to me the Christmas he gave me the set.
If I get you pointing them at anyone, I'll hammer you.
Over two hundred years we've been here in this place.
Just a few fields, a bit of fishing on the river, the orchard and
some bog above on the hill.
Father to son.
Hickson's place is bigger.
Sammy had a great eye for cattle ... and the good-looking girls.
A great roving eye. Hahaha.
Father to son.
Wasn't a bit averse to smuggling the stock backwards and
forwards across the border.
Learnt the tos and fros of it from his father.
Aye.
Fathers and sons.
That's the way of it.
We speak our history to our sons.
Our lives, our languages.
I have no one to speak my history to.
No one to talk to about the drains in the lower field or when we
spray the apple trees, Custer's Last Stand or how I wanted to
marry Grace Kelly.
We both wanted to marry Grace Kelly.

We came out of *High Noon* and never said a word as we walked
down the street. Never looked at the girls even. We got on our
bikes and never said a word and then as we pedalled into the
darkness of the country he started to sing.
Do not forsake me O my darling ...

You could never have a woman like that, I said to him, never in a month of Sundays.

... on this our wedding day ...

Never.

Do not forsake me O my darling.

Never.

People like us ...

Do not forsake me ...

Anyway I was right, wasn't I?

She married that French prince.

Oh aye.

Anyway she's a Taig.

I said that to him and he just laughed.

She's an American, he said.

We saw the picture four times.

I could never remember the words of that song ... but he had them all off after the second time we went to it.

Gary Cooper—now there was a lad.

I told the old fellow about that picture, but that was during the bad times back in the fifties and he'd joined the B-Men and had no time to be going to the pictures.

He had his own gun then.

I used to watch him clean it.

I used to look at those cold bullets and think of them slicing through you.

He never let me touch it.

He never cleaned it in front of the girls ... or my mother.

I said to him once ... I think I must have had a bit of drink taken ... yes ... one night I'd been down in the bar with Sammy and some of the lads ... I came back as he was about to go out on patrol. He was standing in the wee hallway looking at himself in the mirror. He held the gun loosely in his hand, like as if he was old Jimmy Stewart and he was looking at himself in the mirror, sort of admiring himself, imagining things in his head.

I said if you had a white horse and a big hat now, you could let on you were going to save the world ... like General Custer ... like King ... not just snooping round the dark roads looking for

41

Fenians.

He lit out with his fist and punched me in the mouth and left the house.

It was the only time he ever hit me.

My lip bled.

I remember the taste of that blood.

I was only joking him.

There's jokes and jokes, my mother said later on.

Do you never think?

The salt water stung my lip and I nearly cried.

Never think.

She handed me a cloth soaked in witch hazel.

That'll keep the swelling down.

You won't be able to kiss your girl for a couple of days.

I didn't have a girl.

I couldn't get Grace Kelly out of my head.

Sammy wasn't bothered.

Sammy played the field.

He had a job as stock man with Colonel Bradley and helped his father out in his spare time ... and in his spare time he went with every girl in the district ... in the county. Maybe even in the province.

I don't know. I lost track of him for a while.

I went to London then.

Wotcher Paddy.

That's what they said to me every morning for four years.

I never came across Grace Kelly in the dance halls in Kilburn.

Wotcher Paddy.

And I just lifted my fist and felled him and I remembered my father's fist when it hit me and I said, I have a name you bloody English bastard and I left the building site and came home.

Billy Maltseed.

This is my home.

I grew like the trees out of this soil.

Seed.

Sammy was married when I came home, with two wee boys.

A nice enough girl, but not ...

Made a mistake and got caught for life.

A life sentence he said to me in the pub one night.

... not Grace ...

I got back into the swing of things quick enough.

I got this job driving the bus for the area board and helped the old man on the side.

I carried the banner then, instead of him, on the Twelfth. I steadied the pole against the wind. My mother brought sandwiches to the Field and a thermos of tea and Sammy brought beer and we had a bit of crack.

It's a funny thing about the Twelfth ... In those days it was a day out ... a celebration. We sang our songs and beat our drums and some old men made speeches.

Flags and drums and streamers, I remember and we chanted the holy names and sang our holy songs. King Billy had brought us freedom, like my father had said.

Was that what we were celebrating?

I don't remember.

I only remember that it was fun and the girls had their best frocks on and Sammy and I drank a lot of beer and had sore heads the next day.

It's not like that now.

It's hard now.

It's angry now.

It's like the day my father hit me now.

Sammy just had the two boys.

One of them is in college ... over there.

I wonder do they call him Paddy?

A life sentence.

Christine was eighteen when I met her ... well, noticed her.

She always says she'd stepped on and off that bus every day for two years before I noticed her.

I'd given up all thoughts of Grace Kelly by then.

Not that Christine wasn't a nice looking girl. She was that, but not ... well not ... She'd never set the world on fire.

This day she went to get on the bus and she didn't have on her uniform.

Miss ... I said to her ... excuse me, miss, this is a school bus and
she burst out laughing and she ran past me and down the bus to
where her friends were sitting and I could hear them all saying
Miss, excuse me Miss to her all the way to the school.

When she was getting off she stopped by me and gave me a smile.
Right enough, she had a great smile and I thought there and
then if I can't have Grace Kelly, I might as well have this instead.

My mother was upset because she wasn't a Presbyterian.

Could you not have found a nice girl from your own church?

Mixed marriages make bad blood.

You'll have trouble with a girl from the C of I.

Airy fairy notions they have.

I never had any bother with her ... only the one.

Barren is such an ugly word.

I never used it to her.

I never said anything unkind to her.

You can get videos of all those old films now, so you can.

That's what I would have done.

I'd have got one each week and we'd have sat there, the son and
I, and we'd have watched them all, like I did with the old man.

Stagecoach.

They Died with Their Boots On.

Gun fight at the OK Corral.

Drums Along the Mohawk.

Destry. Yes. *Destry.*

The picture houses aren't the same these days.

We'd have been happy at home.

The old man could have watched too.

He'd have liked that.

And *High Noon.*

Mustn't forget *High Noon.*

Do not forsake me O my darling.

His voice was sweet.

Was.

His two boys won't come back here now.

They're full of education.

They'll stay over there.

They'll learn a new language.

They'll learn to call people like us Paddy.

I suppose you could say that Christine and I are happy.

Sammy used to fall in here quite a bit, when he'd a few drops taken ... or more than a few drops ... like after the Regiment Christmas party ... he got a pal to drop him off at our gate. We could hear him coming up the path, swearing and singing and falling about ... disturbing the peace. He started hammering on the door.

For God's sake open the door and let that maniac in before he wakens the old man.

On the green grassy slopes of the ...

... and the O'Kanes.

Open up, this is the law.

He had the gun in his hand when I opened the door and I thought for one cold moment he was going to shoot me.

His hand was trembling and he pointed it straight at my belly.

Do not forsake me O my darling.

It was the only thing I could think of doing.

I whispered the words at him.

On this our wedding day.

Do not forsake me O my darling.

He nodded. He handed me the gun.

Good old King Billy, he said.

It was warm from his hand. I put it down on the table by the door and he just fell asleep ... there on the door step. Fell, like a stone to the ground.

We pulled him into the house.

There was no waking him.

He'd had a skinful.

We put him on the couch by the fire and Christine covered him with a blanket.

He's going to feel terrible in the morning, she said.

Poor Sammy.

It's his wife I feel sorry for, she said.

I picked up the gun and looked at it.

It was loaded and ready to fire.

I didn't tell Christine.

I took the bullets out and put them on the table.

I looked at myself in the mirror ... gun held loosely in my hand.

I smiled, straightened up my back, smiled, raised the gun slightly...

Who do you think you are, anyway?

She was standing in the door looking at me.

Gary Cooper? James Stewart? John Wayne?

She didn't look like Grace Kelly, either.

Stop playing stupid games and come to bed.

Of course, he didn't remember a thing next day.

As I drove him home a funny thought entered my head ... I wondered what would have happened if he'd gone to the wrong house. If he'd gone to the O'Kanes house up the road.

Just the two houses there are out here.

Just the two ...

I'm the man with the gun around here now.

Aye. I have it here in my pocket.

Self-defence they say.

Carry it with you at all times they say.

Wouldn't do you much good here.

Didn't save Sammy.

I don't suppose he had it with him.

He was down in his bottom field loading a sick cow into his trailer when they got him.

Fifteen bullets into his body the report said ...

A year ago that was.

That was a Sunday too.

Like today.

The Sabbath.

I miss him yet.

My pal.

That wee farm of his is up for sale.

The lads didn't want it and she's gone away back to Enniskillen.

You couldn't expect her to live there on her own.

Not after that happened.

There's a bad feeling about the place where someone's been

killed.

That wasn't a very good marriage, right from the start.

I suppose he wasn't the best of husbands.

A life sentence.

She's free of that now.

So is he of course.

You could look at it like that.

Christine and I have a good enough marriage.

But for the one thing.

We never talk about that.

It's hard on her having to look after the old man.

That can't be for long now.

Some old people linger on just to spite you.

His mind's away.

My sisters don't help.

We have the children to mind they say.

True enough. You can't argue with that.

I've no-one to talk to now.

I joined the Regiment after Sammy was shot.

She didn't want me to.

Cried.

I never like to see her cry.

But she doesn't understand.

She couldn't understand.

I might take her away when it's over.

It's hard to get time with the farm and the job and the ...

Yes.

She wanted to go to Vienna a couple of years ago.

What would you do in a place like that?

I've often thought I'd like to go to America.

The West.

See all those places.

Arizona, Texas, the Mohawk River, the Alamo, Little Big Horn.

Just for a week or two.

Stand in those places.

Grace Kelly's dead now.

And Sammy.

She cried.

Duty.

This is my hedge.

I've trimmed this hedge for over twenty years ... and the old man before me.

It's not duty.

God sees into our hearts.

I just thought as I stood there and watched them putting Sammy into the ground ... I'm going to go and get me a big hat and a white horse and a gun.

Silly, I suppose.

This is my hedge.

It's not duty.

My wee fields.

My house with the old man dying and Christine.

Barren.

No matter about that.

I must say that to her one day. No matter.

The holy names keep you safe.

Jimmy Stewart. Gary Cooper. Randolph Scott. Burt Lancaster. Kirk Douglas. General Custer ... Destry ... Billy the Kid ... Billy the King.

Sammy Hickson.

Oh aye, Sammy.

Up there with Grace now, are you Sam?

Pulled a fast one on your pal, did you Sam?

Hahhaha!

Do not forsake me O my darling ...

CHRISTINE

Christine was first performed at the Peacock Theatre, Dublin, in 1989. The role of Christine was played by Rosaleen Linehan. The production was directed by Caroline FitzGerald.

The monologue was later broadcast by BBC Radio Ulster on 20th April, 1989. The role of Christine was played by Stella McCusker and the broadcast was directed by Jeremy Howe.

Aye.

That's it then.

All red up.

Some people would just walk out of a place ... slam the door behind them. Aye.

There's ones like that ... would never give a second thought to the dust ... to the grime.

Aye.

Grime.

I couldn't do a thing like that.

I couldn't let strangers come in here and find things to point the finger at.

Strangers.

God knows, there's been enough of them around in the last couple of weeks.

Gawkers.

Every day I've watched them, driving down the wee lane, slowing down their cars when they get to the gate.

A couple of them stopped, stopped dead there by the gate and stuck their heads out of the windows.

I was affronted.

Curiosity killed the cat.

I wanted to open my door and shout that down the path at them.

Curiosity killed the cat.

My mother always used to say that to us when we were kids.

I didn't believe her.

I never saw too many dead cats around the place.

I remember my brother once shot one with an air gun.

Killed it.

That wasn't very nice.

He didn't realise ... you know about death and that. He didn't mean to hurt it, you see. Just thought ... I don't know what he thought, but I know he didn't mean to harm it.

He never touched the air gun after that.

My mother cried when she saw the cat.

That upset him.

She never said a word to him ... only cried.

Soft.

He was quite soft, my brother.

I don't mean soft in the head ... oh no, nothing like that ... just he was a soft man.

I haven't seen a lot of him over the years.

His wife's a decent woman, but they don't have much time to spare. She works, and what with that and the wains she's tired. You know ... washed out.

Fair dos to them, they came down to the funeral.

Aye. Fair dos.

I don't know how he ... oh yes ... cats ... funny the way your mind works. It flies around ... or maybe it's just mine.

It's probably just mine. I've never been what you'd call clever.

I don't understand a lot of things. I don't seem to be able to control my mind at all.

I don't get much out of books so I don't. I never did. Never had much time for books.

I like the telly, though.

I like to see people's faces. Here in the room. Sometimes it is full of people's faces.

You'd never really be alone if you had the telly. That's what I always used to think.

It's not like that though.

They don't notice you, those people there.

They don't care about you.

Why should they, after all?

They have their own lives to lead ... their own problems.

I mean to say, some of them run the world.

It's odd to see the people who run the world right here in your room.

Their faces say nothing to me.

I wonder sometimes how they carry all that stuff around in their heads.

Figures and that.

Long words.

Notions.

Information.

All that information.

They make it all sound so important ... and then I feel foolish because I don't understand it ... I mean about the Middle East and that ... I don't understand ... I don't suppose it matters whether I do or not.

It's a funny thing, people's shoes don't creak nowadays.

When I was a child, people's shoes used to squeak.

It means they haven't paid for them, my mother used to say.

She was from the south, my mother.

You couldn't believe everything she said.

I'm sure that Mrs. Thatcher's shoes creak.

I don't know why. I always get that feeling when I look at her on the telly, I think to myself, I bet your shoes creak.

I said it to Billy once ...

To Billy.

He howled.

He laughed a lot.

He liked to laugh.

Billy.

Easy amused.

I used to say that to him.

Billy Maltseed, you're easy amused.

My name is Christine.

Billy and Christine.

We had that written in silver letters on our wedding invitations. It looked very smart ... and bells ... you know sort of ringing sideways ... and a couple of wee angels ... lovely.

Yes.

That was a lovely day.

I have the pictures ... everyone smiling.

Only my granny wouldn't come up from Carlow. She said she might be shot.

God, but we laughed at that.

I was a bit sad, though.

I loved my granny.

You'd think she'd have taken the chance.

A bit too old for adventures, Billy said.

53

He never met her.
He'd have liked her.
A gas woman. Old but.
She'd have made him howl.
My mother wanted her up too.
In all the years my mother lived up here, my granny never came up once to visit her.
We had to go down there.
Not that I minded, but my mother did.
Do you think we have horns or something she said to her once?
Gran used to laugh at my voice ... not unkindly you know ... just the odd wee joke.
My mother never lost her southern voice, but I couldn't help the way I talked.
I said that to her. *Granny, I can't help the way I talk.*
Wisha, I know love.
She said that.
Wisha.
Very old fashioned that. No one says that sort of thing now.
Wisha.
You never know when you're happy.
I often wonder if Mrs. Thatcher's happy ... or the Queen. I don't like the glasses she has to wear ... they make her look cross.
I love to see her in the crown and all that, but those glasses spoil it.
I wonder if she knows.
I wonder if she watches herself on telly. Perhaps she doesn't have the time.
My granny said she could remember Queen Victoria, but Billy always said she must have been pulling my leg. He said she was old, but not that old.

Old Queen Vic,
Walking with a stick,
Run or she'll catch you.
Quick, quick, quick.

Not very respectable really.

She used to shout that at me when I was wee.

Down there in Carlow.

I wrote to my cousin Doreen, she was one of my bridesmaids ... well I wrote to her the other week and told her I might come down to live near her. She's married and has two wee boys, well they were wee when I last saw them, they must be ... getting into their teens now ... her husband's in the bank in Kilkenny. A nice enough fellow. I went down once to visit them, several years ago. It was Billy insisted I go ... to take my mind off things, he said. It was the summer I went to the hospital to have the tests. Doreen had the two wee fellows then, little pets they were.

It made me sad to see them. Isn't that a silly thing to say?

I never had the heart to tell Billy what they said at the hospital ... I just let him think it was my fault ...

You know the way some men are ... they get very hurt about that sort of thing, ashamed. I'm not sure why. Men feel more ashamed than women. I think so.

That's why I never told him the truth.

It was hard sometimes not to let it come bursting out ... you know when we had a wee row or something.

Old Mrs. Maltseed always went on about it.

Well Christine, no news for us yet?

I just used to smile at her, but sometimes I felt I could do her an injury.

She was a rough sort of a woman ... right enough she'd had a hard life, out here in these hills, managing, trying to make ends meet, keep a look on things.

Never a speck of dust there was in this house. You could have eaten your dinner off the floor.

No amenities in those days either.

We put the bathroom in ... Imagine that! No bathroom and a toilet out in the yard when we came here ... and that not all that long ago ... well I mean to say it's within living memory!

I couldn't live like that, I said to Billy.

You may be used to it, but I'm not ... and I had the old man to look after and all ... all that washing extra.

Sheets. Every day there were sheets and his pyjamas ... that was later on of course. Not to begin with. I didn't know then the way things were going to go with him.

To give him his due, he worked hard when he was able.

I must say Billy was very good ... he got that job with the area board driving the school bus and fitted it in with the farm ... he was never lazy, never one for sitting round and letting things get the better of him.

We never did anyone any harm.

That's what I said in my letter to Doreen.

I couldn't understand why she didn't want me to come.

A short holiday perhaps, she said, *after all the fuss has died down ... but then you'll have to stand on your own feet.*

I didn't ask to stand on hers, did I? Haha ... Haha.

It was like as if she thought I had some dreadful disease that I was going to spread around, contaminate her family, those two nice boys ... Fred ... Kilkenny City ... the Allied Irish Bank ... the whole country maybe.

Contaminate.

I wouldn't want to go there if she felt like that.

I wrote and told her that.

We never did anyone any harm.

We kept ourselves to ourselves.

I'm not saying I didn't have any friends ... I did. I had friends all right.

We didn't say much to each other, but we were friends.

It's quite lonely here in the winter.

The nights seem very long.

Billy was good company, I have to say that and there was the telly.

I had a good friend who was ...

Dolores O'Kane.

Lives just down the road.

The bungalow down the hill with the red roof.

He was cool enough, but I liked her.

We had the same problem ... the father-in-law.

You can laugh.

That's what we used to do ... have a laugh. You have to have a laugh from time to time. Not at anyone's expense of course, just at things ... you know, things in general.

That's what we used to do, have a cup of tea and a laugh.

She has kids ... that's a help ... It makes you look into the future ... see some ... hope?

Perhaps I shouldn't say hope.

I think I'd feel some hope if I had children.

Maybe not.

We always used to talk about the children we would have.

Well, in the early days we did.

Later on I thought of adopting ... but then I wondered would I love the child?

Could I give him what he needed?

Would he love me ... and Billy.

You never know where a baby comes from ... an adopted one I mean, of course.

It sounds silly, but my mother always used to say to us ... don't put that in your mouth, you never know where it's been.

I felt a bit like that about adopting.

I think Billy was the same.

I used to talk to Dolores about it ... that was after I knew ... after I'd been to the hospital. I never told her that I was all right. I thought that wouldn't be fair. She might mention it to someone and then it might get back to Billy.

You shouldn't trust people too much.

I suppose it's as well, under the circumstances, that we didn't have any children.

Think how they'd be now.

Orphans.

No ... they wouldn't be orphans ... they'd have me.

I'd stay here if I had children.

I'd work my fingers to the bone.

My mother always said a bit of hard work never hurt anyone.

Mind you, you see others destroyed by the lack of it.

I'd have loved a wee girl.

Some nights I used to hold him, close in my arms and rock him.

If I shut my eyes I could imagine it was a ...

He never knew that was what I was thinking.

So many things we didn't say to each other.

I suppose everyone's the same.

Filled with secrets.

The doctor said just to tell him to go along to the clinic.

It's probably very easy to deal with Mrs. Maltseed, he said.

He was nice.

I didn't have the heart to tell Billy.

He liked to play the big guy. You know ... tough guy Billy Maltseed.

That was what he liked about the Lodge ... all those men ... preening themselves. I used to laugh to myself when I saw them, beating their drums, marching, flags, all that sort of thing.

I used to wonder what they were like inside, under the clothes and the sashes.

I said to him once, turn a bowler hat upside down and guess what you could use it for?

He wasn't all that amused.

We are not amused, my mother used to say when I did something silly.

We are not amused.

I put the sashes in the coffins with them ... His and the old man's.

I didn't want to see them again. I thought the minister might say something, but he didn't. Maybe he didn't know.

My mother was Church of Ireland.

I don't think I'm anything at all.

I used to love the Church of Ireland when I was young.

Oh, let the earth bless the Lord, yea, let it praise Him and magnify Him forever.

That one I liked.

Oh Ananias, Azarias and Miseal, bless ye the Lord ...

They don't sing things like that in the Presbyterian Church.

Praise Him and magnify Him forever.

I asked Billy once why they didn't and he said ... we did away with that sort of rubbish a long time ago. We speak direct to the Lord. That's what he said.

I didn't believe him.

I was lonely for Ananias, Azarias and Miseal.

Whoever they were.

I never knew who they were, but I could see them, walking with me, their great wings folded behind them.

Great feathery wings.

I miss their company.

Matthew Mark Luke and John bless the bed that I lie on.

Every night before I go to sleep I say that.

And if I die before I wake ...

I didn't tell Billy.

... I pray the Lord my soul to take.

I don't see any harm in saying that.

My mother used to whisper that to me as she tucked me in, and then she kissed me ... now you're all right she'd say ... they'll mind you.

They have to.

I suppose.

I'm not complaining.

They've their work cut out for them, minding all the people who say that last thing at night.

Even when I held him in my arms and pretended he was my little baby ... even then I used to sing that in my head ... *Matthew Mark ... and if I die before I wake, I pray the Lord my soul to take ...* He never knew.

He thought I thought like him, believed like him.

Listen ... you can hear Dolores' children playing in the field.

I used to give them apples from our apple tree ... They had none of their own.

We had pears, too, and greengages. The old man planted the greengage tree at the end of the war.

The children used to come and steal fruit at night.

They enjoyed that much more than me giving them fruit.

That's children for you!

I was going to train as a teacher and then I met Billy.

Where's the point he said?

My mother had taken the cancer then and was weak in herself.

She just said suit yourself child, but don't forget the five wits God gave you.

I never knew what they were.

She'd have liked me to be a teacher all right. I knew that.

I could see it in her face.

Billy was such fun.

I can't wait forever, he said.

There's plenty of good fish in the sea, my mother said, but I liked Billy.

We never had a row, in all those years. Well hardly a row, not like other people have.

Twenty.

Next May.

Yes.

Twenty.

He said he'd take me away for a holiday.

To celebrate, you know.

Twenty years is a good long time.

He got those books from the travel agent.

I threw them in the bin the other day.

Where's the point now?

I wouldn't want to go on my own.

Dolores went to Spain last year.

She said it was great ... as long as you didn't touch the food.

I didn't come from near the sea.

It frightened me.

I suppose it's what you're used to.

I thought Switzerland would be nice, but he said it was a bit expensive ... or Vienna. That's the place where they have those lovely horses.

I've seen them on the telly.

They dance.

I'd like to have gone and seen those horses ... but that was about the time the old man got bad and we couldn't go anywhere.

I thought we should have put him in the hospital ... he'd have been well looked after there.

Dolores' father-in-law is in the hospital.

They go and visit him once a week. She brings him biscuits.

He likes ginger biscuits. He dips them in his tea.

My mother never let me do that.

Your teeth will rot in your head if you eat slops like that, she used to say.

He didn't like wearing his teeth.

Dolores used to have a terrible time with him when he was in the house, trying to get him to wear his teeth.

Billy wouldn't hear of it.

My father's going into no home.

We can mind him.

We!

I laughed a bit when he said that ... inside myself of course.

He hasn't long for it, we can manage. He said that to the minister. There was a nice small place run by the church for old people like him. But Billy had his mind made up.

I went up to the hospital one day with Dolores, when she went to visit. There were six of them all in the one room. I think he'd have liked that. A bit of company. The nurses seemed decent enough. Jokey you know.

He's still going strong.

Maybe old Mr. Maltseed would still be going strong if ...

If ifs and ands were pots and pans there'd be no room for tinkers.

She used to say that too.

If ...

It was the shock that killed him.

If only ...

I had to tell him ...

There wasn't anyone else really.

I thought of asking the minister, but I didn't think it would be right.

Unkind to have such words said by a stranger.

There's been Maltseeds in this house for over two hundred years.

I suppose some people thought it was time for a change.

That's a joke, in case you don't recognise it.

I don't really mean that.

I said it to Dolores the day after the two funerals.

She didn't think it was funny.

Then, of course, I realised I shouldn't say that sort of thing to her.

She's been a good neighbour.

A good friend, no matter what people may say.

There are times you should keep your mouth shut.

Hold your tongue.

When my mother used to say that to me, I'd to put my tongue out of my mouth and pinch it between my thumb and finger ... like this I'm sure you remember doing the same thing.

She'd laugh.

Rapscallion, she'd say.

I never heard anyone else use that word.

It's a great word, isn't it?

Rapscallion.

It's a very cheerful word.

If I'da had kids, I'd have called them ...

Dolores says that everything is sent by God.

I can't see it like that.

Why would he have me in such sorrow?

What have I ever done to him?

I am such a small person. I can't believe he can even see me when he looks down from the sky. I'm not like those people you see on the telly.

I asked Dolores that ... she didn't know the answer either ... unless of course it's because I'm a Protestant ... but that can't be right, because so many others suffer too.

I didn't ask the Minister because I don't think he likes me very much.

I get that feeling from him.

I went to him the time Billy first said he was going to join the Regiment.

I asked him to have a word with Billy ... to say something to him ... but he wouldn't. He said he thought it was a very good thing that Billy should join ...

I said to him ... but, Reverend, the Bible says we mustn't kill people. I didn't say it right out like that, but that was what I meant.

Dear Mrs. Maltseed, he spoke in a sort of dry little voice, *I hope it will never come to that. I'm sure,* he said, *that Billy will not allow himself to be carried beyond the bounds of duty by bigotry or over-zealousness.*

I remember that ... *over-zealousness.*

Isn't it funny the way some people talk.

I suppose he got a word like that from the Bible.

The Good Book, he used to call it.

They try to hide things sometimes in the way they talk.

I think our Minister's a bit fond of the sound of his own voice.

Dry little voice, like it hurt him to speak.

I suppose I could always go back to the Church of Ireland now.

I hadn't thought of that before.

Oh Ananias, Azarias and ...

I'll have to get a job.

... Miseal.

The money for the house won't last forever.

Maybe they'll come back and walk beside me.

I never had a job.

It's a nice wee house, after all we've done to it ... and fifty acres.

No-one wants to live around here.

Dolores' husband offered to take the land ... but who'd buy the house without the land.

It's been well-looked after all these years.

People are afraid now.

People like us are afraid.

That was why he joined the Regiment.

A lot of his pals joined it years ago, but it wasn't till Sam Hickson was shot he decided to join himself.

Where's the point I asked him?

I mean he wasn't cut out to be a soldier.

And why bring trouble on yourself.

Why be a hero?

He was wild upset when Sam was killed

Sam was a good friend of his.

They'd went to school together.

They were in the same Lodge.

He had a bit of a problem with the drink and he spent a few nights here when he was too full to go home to his wife. When he wouldn't have been able to find his way home to his wife, put it like that. But he was decent enough.

Lived down near the lake.

(Oh ye whales and things that move in the waters, bless ye the Lord.)

I didn't tell anyone about Billy joining the Regiment ... Like my cousin Doreen, I never told her.

They have odd notions in the south ... but then she saw it in the papers and she was all upset. That's one of the reasons they don't want me down there ... at least I think it is.

I didn't tell Dolores either ... but she just said to me one day ... came right out with it ...

Is your Billy in the Regiment?

Just like that, I was over having a cup of tea in her kitchen.

Oh aye ... he is.

I couldn't tell her a lie.

Part-time, I said.

She never said a word.

She just gave me a funny look.

There's no harm in it, I said.

I didn't think there was any harm in it.

I don't think Billy thought there was any harm in it either.

A duty. Aye.

A duty.

I think they had a bit of crack too.

Like wee boys.

I didn't think your Billy'd do a thing like that.

She said to me about a week later.

Like what?

I asked, but I knew.

You know well, she said.

It's road blocks and the like, I said.

She gave me another funny look and passed me a piece of cake.

She's very good at making cakes.

She brought me down one of her fruit cakes the day before the funeral.

Rich dark fruit cake she makes ... like my mother used to.

Old fashioned.

You don't get them like that in the shops.

My mother never bought a cake in her life.

Nothing would have persuaded her.

The day I can't make a cake myself is the day we stop eating cakes.

Of course, in her last few months, she didn't want to eat nothing at all.

Turned right off her food.

Faded away.

Big eyes staring out of her head and she couldn't keep her teeth in her mouth.

I was affronted every time I saw her.

O ye children of men, bless ye the Lord.

She was a good woman.

My heart was broken watching her die.

I suppose you could say Billy was saved that.

He didn't know what hit him.

That's what the doctors said anyway.

I wonder.

It was a wonder that none of the kids in the bus were injured.

I suppose whoever done it wouldn't have cared.

I shouldn't say that.

I shouldn't feel like that, but sometimes I can't help it.

I have asked God to fill me full of charity, but he hasn't had time yet.

I had to identify the body.

That seemed so silly to me, didn't everyone know that it was Billy Maltseed drove the school bus.

I didn't want to see him.

I said it to them, but they paid no heed.

It's the law missus.

It seems a silly law to me ... to persecute someone like that.

I didn't want to see him at all. I just wanted him to be nailed up in the coffin so that I could remember him, held tight in my arms like a baby.

I can't see that any more.

The other picture gets in the way.

I wondered and wondered whether to tell the old man, but I was afraid that with all the fuss going on and the people in and out and the press banging on the door he might get troubled. He used to get troubled and cry when he didn't understand what was going on.

So I went up to his room and I told him.

I don't think he understood to begin with, he just lay there smiling and googling ... That's what I used to call it ... googling. He used to wave his head from side to side and make this funny noise.

It meant something, but you had to try and work out what it was. *Would you stop your googling*, I'd say to him sometimes, but only when I was tired, or when there was something good on the telly and I wanted away.

But he must have known what I said because, half an hour after, he took this terrible turn. By the time the doctor came he was gone.

When Dolores came round with the cake I told her about it.

Two for the price of one, I said.

I shouldn't have.

Sometimes a little joke lifts your spirits.

She looked most upset.

You shouldny say things like that, she said

Why don't you have a good cry, let it all come out, she said.

I couldn't.

I just couldn't cry ... not because I didn't want to, just the tears wouldn't come out of my eyes.

Billy's sisters cried. They came to the funeral and bawled all over the place.

I never shed a tear.

I felt terrible.

You're being very brave, Mrs. Maltseed.

Rotten, dry little voice and he spoke his prayers in that rotten voice and I still had dry eyes and all the officers and Orange men and the MP were there and they all spoke to me and my eyes were bursting out of my head with pain and I still couldn't cry.

You probably saw the funeral on the telly.

I sat and watched it that evening on the news after everyone had gone home ... how strange I thought to see myself there on the telly.

I really do exist, that's me there, walking, standing, shaking hands ... that's me. I am a real person.

If I'd had a video, I'd have taped it.

I could have looked at it over and over again. I could have said Christine Maltseed, that's you there on the telly with the eyes bursting out of your head with pain.

... and then I cried, when I saw myself there with all those people.

Dolores didn't come to the funeral.

I could hardly have expected her to.

But she's been very good to me ever since.

I mean she pops in every day to see if I'm alright. Brings me little bits of this and that ... some cold ham, a bit of pie.

She's a good woman.

I'll miss her.

I'll miss this place.

My brother's found me a wee place in Belfast.

Just big enough to swing a cat, he says.

I'm a bit afraid of Belfast, but as my mother would have said you can get used to anything if you try.

I thought I might try for a job in Marks & Spencer, somewhere nice like that.

What with the compensation and the bit of money from the house, I'll be alright for a while.

I don't like leaving Billy.

I hope he won't mind.

After all why should he—he'll have Ananias, Azarias and Miseal for company now.

Dolores says she'll pop in to see me whenever she comes up to Belfast.

That'll be nice.

She can tell me how things are going on here.

I gave each one of her kids a pound this morning.

Dolores said I shouldn't have.

They seemed pleased enough.

I said to them now you'll be able to steal the apples in peace.

They smiled but I don't think they thought it was very funny.
I think it's some friend of Dolores' husband is buying the place.
I heard that round.
That'll be nice for the children. They'll have other kids to play with.
It's a bit lonely out here.
Oh Ananias, Azarias and Miseal, bless ye the Lord,
Praise him and magnify him for ever.
It's time I went.
The bus passes the end of the lane in ten minutes:
I wouldn't want to miss it.
I hope I haven't taken up too much of your time.
Goodbye.

Other Plays from Lagan Press

Joseph Tomelty
All Souls' Night & Other Plays
edited and introduced by Damian Smyth
ISBN: 1 873687 04 4
216 pp, £4.95 pbk

Best known as a stage and film actor and as the creator of *The McCooeys*—Northern Ireland's 1940s radio soap which made him a household name in his native place—Joseph Tomelty is also a novelist, short-story writer and, above all, a playwright.

This book, selected by poet and critic, Damian Smyth, gathers for the first time into one volume four major Tomelty plays— the sombre and deeply sad *All Souls' Night* (1948), the lyric *The Singing Bird* (1948), the serio-comic *April in Assagh* (1953) and the controversial *The End House* (1944).

All Souls' Night, set in a dark, passionless world on the east coast of Ulster, is his most critically-acclaimed play. Dealing with poverty, meanness of soul and a mother's consuming greed, it has been described as the best play written in the north of Ireland. It is counterpointed by *April in Assagh*, a play set in a fantastical townland, which is funny and satirical with a dark core of foreboding and published here for the first time. *The End House* creates a Belfast of urban violence after the model of O'Casey. *The Singing Bird*, written for radio in 1948 and later adapted for television, starring Tomelty himself, is a beautiful, pastoral tale of 'a gentle madness'.

Together, these plays provide an indisensable insight into the workings of the double-side imagination of Tomelty's place— on the one hand deeply obsessive and corrosive, on the other witty, meditative and happy and all with an exhilarating muscular lyricism.

Martin Lynch
Three Plays
edited by Damian Smyth
ISBN: 1 873687 60 5
200pp, £4.95 pbk

Martin Lynch has been a significant figure in Irish drama
since the late 1970s when *They Are Taking Down the Barricades*
gave expression to contemporary Belfast working-class life.
Rooted among the political and imaginative forces bearing
upon and emerging from both northern communities, Lynch
explored those forces with humour, anger and compassion.

Having committed himself to the values of community-based
drama, he wrote a string of popular successes throughout the
1980s. Marked by an accurate ear for dialogue and a pungent
wit, the plays chalked out a territory securely his own. Out of
this committment have come also three of the most
important plays in the last twenty-five years from the north of
Ireland—*Dockers, The Interrogation of Ambrose Fogarty* and
Pictures of Tomorrow.

Dockers is a boisterous recreation of working-class life in
Belfast's famed Sailortown district. Reminiscent of Dario Fo
but rigorously rooted in the sadness of real political conflict,
The Interrogation of Ambrose Fogarty is a most vivid, pointed and
funny play dealing with the ironies and absurdities of police
detention. With *Pictures of Tomorrow,* Lynch attempts to deal
with the disillusion of left-wing ideals in the wake of the
collapse of communism, against the poignant backdrop of
the Spanish Civil War, a conflict loaded with Irish resonances.

These plays, available for the first time, establish Martin
Lynch as a leading Irish playwright of his generation.

To order these or other Lagan Press titles, write to:
Lagan Press, PO Box 110 Belfast BT12 4AB
(post and packaging free)